Table of Contents

From Chaos to Clarity:
A Comprehensive Guide to Organizing Every Facet of Your Life

SUE NEUMANN

How to Organize All Aspects Of Life With Easy-to-Follow Tips & Tricks

FROM CHAOS TO CLARITY: A COMPREHENSIVE GUIDE TO ORGANIZING EVERY FACET OF YOUR LIFE

Sue Neumann

Copyright © 2023
Sue Neumann

Chapter 1: Introduction

The Beauty of Organization

In the vast tapestry of life, where threads of events, emotions, and experiences intertwine, there lies a subtle yet profound art: the art of organization. It's not just about neatly arranged books on a shelf or a color-coded calendar; it's about the harmony that emerges when every piece of our life finds its rightful place. The beauty of organization is akin to a symphony where each instrument plays its part, creating a melody that resonates with peace, clarity, and purpose.

Many believe that organization is a trait you're either born with or without. However, the truth is far more empowering. Organization is a skill, a habit cultivated over time. It's an ongoing journey of understanding oneself, recognizing the chaos, and then methodically transforming it into order. And like any art form, it requires patience, practice, and a touch of creativity.

Why This Book? The Promise of a Simplified Life

In the age of information overload, where our attention is pulled in a million directions, and our to-do lists seem never-ending, the quest for organization has never been more critical. Yet, amidst the hustle and bustle, many of us feel lost, overwhelmed by the sheer magnitude of tasks and responsibilities that life throws our way. That's where this book comes into play.

"Mastering Life's Chaos: Organizing Every Aspect with Simple Tips & Tricks" is not just another self-help book. It's a compass, a guide, a friend that will hold your hand as you navigate the labyrinth of life. Whether you're drowning in clutter, struggling to manage your time, or seeking peace of mind, this book promises to light the way.

The chapters that follow are meticulously crafted, drawing from timeless wisdom, personal experiences, and modern techniques. They delve deep into various facets of life, offering actionable insights to help you find order in disorder. From decluttering your living space to managing your finances, from cultivating mindfulness to nurturing relationships, this book covers it all.

But why should you embark on this journey of organization? The answer is simple: an organized life is a simplified life. It's a life where you're in control, where every day feels purposeful, and where joy isn't overshadowed by stress. It's a life where you can breathe easy, knowing that you're making the most of every moment.

As you turn the pages, remember that organization is not about perfection. It's about progress. It's about recognizing the beauty in both order and chaos and finding a balance that works for you. So, with an open heart and a curious mind, let's embark on this transformative journey together. Welcome to "Mastering Life's Chaos." Let the adventure begin!

Chapter 2: The Foundations of Organization

The Psychology Behind Clutter

At the heart of every cluttered space, be it a room or a mind, lies a story. Take, for instance, Sarah, a talented writer with a penchant for collecting antique typewriters. Over the years, her collection grew, filling every nook and cranny of her home. While each piece held sentimental value, the sheer volume began to overwhelm her living space. The clutter wasn't just physical; it began to weigh on her mind, stifling her creativity.

Psychologists have long studied the impact of clutter on our mental well-being. Clutter, in essence, is a manifestation of unmade decisions. Every item we hold onto, unsure of its place or purpose, represents a decision deferred. Over time, these accumulate, leading to feelings of anxiety, stress, and even guilt. A study from the Princeton University Neuroscience Institute found that clutter competes for our attention, reducing our ability to focus and process information.

However, the relationship between our psyche and clutter isn't one-sided. Often, our internal chaos manifests externally. Emotional turmoil, unresolved traumas, or even the fear of scarcity can lead us to cling to material possessions as a form of comfort or control.

The Benefits of an Organized Life

Imagine waking up in a room where everything has its place. The sunlight filters through clear windows, casting a warm glow on a neatly made bed. Your favorite book awaits on the nightstand, and there's not a stray sock in sight. This isn't just a scene from a home decor magazine; it's a glimpse into the life of James, a once-chronic hoarder who embraced the power of organization.

The benefits James reaped were multifold. On a tangible level, his living space became more functional and aesthetically pleasing. But the deeper transformations were internal. With less physical clutter to navigate, James found he had more time and energy. His sleep improved, his stress levels plummeted, and he rediscovered passions long buried under piles of junk.

An organized life, as James discovered, is synonymous with freedom. Freedom from the shackles of excess, freedom to pursue passions, and freedom to live in the present. It paves the way for improved mental health, increased productivity, and a profound sense of accomplishment.

The Pillars of Organization: Simplicity, Consistency, and Mindfulness

At the core of every organized life lie three foundational pillars: Simplicity, Consistency, and Mindfulness.

- Simplicity: Marie, a high-flying executive, once boasted a wardrobe that would put celebrities to shame. Yet, every morning, she faced the 'I have nothing to wear' conundrum. The epiphany came during a trip to Japan, where she encountered the minimalist lifestyle. Inspired, Marie adopted the mantra of 'less is more.' She downsized her wardrobe, keeping only pieces that she truly loved and wore. The result? Quicker decisions, less stress, and a newfound appreciation for quality over quantity.

- Consistency: Raj, a schoolteacher, had a habit of misplacing his keys. Every morning was a frantic search, often making him late. The solution was deceptively simple: a designated key bowl by the door. But the magic lay in the consistent act of placing the keys in the bowl every single time. Over weeks, this small act transformed into a habit, eliminating the morning chaos.

● Mindfulness: Ana, a busy mother of three, often found herself purchasing duplicate items, forgetting what she already had at home. The shift came when she began practicing mindfulness, being present during every task, be it shopping or organizing. This conscious awareness reduced impulsive purchases and fostered a deeper connection with her surroundings.

In the grand tapestry of life, organization isn't just about decluttering spaces; it's about decluttering the soul. It's about recognizing the stories our possessions tell, understanding the emotions they evoke, and curating a life that truly reflects who we are. As we journey through this book, let these foundational pillars guide the way, serving as touchstones in our quest for order amidst chaos.

Chapter 3: Organizing Your Physical Spaces

14

Home Sweet Organized Home

The home is often described as an extension of oneself—a sanctuary where memories are made, dreams are nurtured, and souls find rest. Yet, for many, this sanctuary can quickly become a source of stress. Picture Lisa, a passionate artist with a flair for collecting unique art supplies. Over time, her home transformed into a maze of paints, brushes, and canvases. While each item was a testament to her passion, the clutter began to stifle her creativity.

● Decluttering 101: The Kon Mari Method & Beyond

○ Introduced by Marie Kondo, the Kon Mari method revolves around a simple principle: retain only those items that "spark joy." Lisa embarked on this journey, holding each item, gauging its emotional resonance, and parting with those that no longer served her. The result? A curated collection that not only simplified her space but also rekindled her artistic fire.

○ But decluttering isn't one-size-fits-all. While some, like Lisa, resonate with the emotional approach of Kon Mari, others might prefer the pragmatic Four-Box Method: Keep, Toss, Donate, Relocate. The key is to find a method that aligns with one's personal ethos.

● Room-by-Room Guide: From Bedrooms to Basements

○ The bedroom, often deemed a personal sanctuary, can benefit from the "BED" technique: **B**egin with decluttering, **E**stablish zones (sleep, work, relax), and **D**edicate spaces for each item. Take Mark, a freelancer who transformed his chaotic bedroom into a multi-functional space, with clear zones for sleep, work, and relaxation.

○ Basements, notorious for being dumping grounds, can be tackled with the "Three S's": **S**ort (categorize items), **S**tore (use clear bins and labels), and **S**ustain (regularly revisit and declutter).

● The Magic of Storage Solutions

○ Innovative storage solutions can be game changers. Consider Nina, a shoe enthusiast. Instead of piling boxes, she opted for clear shoe drawers, allowing easy access and visibility. Similarly, vertical storage, like wall-mounted pegboards or over-the-door organizers, can maximize space while keeping items accessible.

Workspace Wonders

In today's digital age, the line between home and office often blurs. A well-organized workspace can be the catalyst for productivity and creativity. Reflect on Alex, a digital nomad whose work took him to various corners of his home, from the dining table to the couch. The lack of a dedicated workspace impacted his focus and efficiency.

● The Minimalist Desk

○ Inspired by minimalist workspaces on Pinterest, Alex created a clutter-free desk. He adopted the "One In, One Out" rule: for every new item added, one had to go. This ensured that only essential items graced his workspace, reducing distractions.

● Digital Decluttering: Organizing Your Computer & Online Spaces

○ Beyond physical clutter, digital chaos can be equally overwhelming. Alex began with his computer desktop, categorizing files into folders and regularly backing up to cloud storage. He also embraced email management tools, creating folders, and setting aside dedicated times for email checks, reducing constant digital interruptions.

● The Power of a Productive Workspace

○ Ergonomics played a pivotal role in Alex's workspace transformation. Investing in a comfortable chair and adjustable desk, coupled with regular breaks, boosted his productivity and well-being.

In the realm of physical spaces, organization is more than mere aesthetics. It's about creating environments that nurture our passions, fuel our productivity, and soothe our souls. Whether it's the comforting embrace of a well-organized home or the invigorating energy of a clutter-free workspace, the magic lies in the balance between form and function. As we journey through life, let our spaces be a reflection of our aspirations, a testament to our journeys, and a sanctuary for our dreams.

Chapter 4: Organizing Your Time

The Art of Time Management

Time, the ever-elusive resource, flows like a river—constant, unyielding, and often slipping through our fingers. Consider Amelia, a young entrepreneur juggling her startup, family commitments, and personal passions. Each day felt like a race against the clock, leaving her exhausted and unfulfilled.

● Understanding Your Time: The Time Audit

○ Amelia's transformation began with a simple yet profound exercise: the Time Audit. For a week, she meticulously logged every activity, from work meetings to scrolling through social media. The revelations were eye-opening. Those "quick" Instagram breaks totaled hours, while essential tasks were rushed or overlooked.

○ A Time Audit, as Amelia discovered, offers a mirror to our habits, highlighting areas of inefficiency and opportunities for realignment.

● Prioritizing Tasks: The Eisenhower Box & The Pomodoro Technique

○ Armed with insights from her audit, Amelia turned to the Eisenhower Box, a matrix segregating tasks into four categories: Urgent & Important, Not Urgent & Important, Urgent & Not Important, and Neither. This visual tool helped her discern between genuine priorities and deceptive distractions.

○ For focused work sessions, Amelia embraced the Pomodoro Technique. Working in 25-minute bursts, followed by a 5-minute break, she found her productivity soaring and burnout diminishing.

● The Miracle Morning: Starting Your Day Right

○ Inspired by Hal Elrod's "The Miracle Morning," Amelia crafted a morning routine encompassing Silence (meditation), Affirmations, Visualization, Exercise, Reading, and Scribing (journaling). This sacred hour set a positive, purposeful tone for her day, amplifying her energy and focus.

Planning for Success

In the grand symphony of life, each day is a note, each week a melody, and each year a composition. Crafting this symphony requires intention, foresight, and a touch of creativity.

● Analog vs. Digital: Finding the Right Planner

○ While Amelia appreciated the convenience of digital calendars, she yearned for the tactile joy of pen and paper. Her solution? A hybrid approach. She used digital tools for reminders and syncing across devices, while an analog planner captured her thoughts, goals, and reflections.

○ Whether you're Team Digital, Team Analog, or somewhere in between, the key is consistency. Regularly updating and reviewing your planner ensures alignment with your goals and adaptability to life's ever-changing rhythms.

The Power of Routines: Morning, Evening, and Weekend Editions

○ Beyond her Miracle Morning, Amelia established evening rituals. A digital detox an hour before sleep, reflecting on her day, and light reading ensured restful slumber. Weekends, meanwhile, were reserved for planning the week ahead, self-care, and quality family time.

● Time Blocking: The Secret to Uninterrupted Productivity

○ Taking a leaf from Elon Musk's playbook, Amelia adopted time blocking. Segmenting her day into dedicated blocks—be it for deep work, administrative tasks, or leisure—she ensured a holistic approach to time management, balancing productivity with relaxation.

Time, as Amelia realized, isn't just about hours and minutes; it's about moments and memories. Organizing our time is a dance—a dance of priorities, passions, and purpose. It's about crafting days that resonate with intention, weeks that echo with progress, and years that reflect a life well-lived. As we waltz through the pages of our lives, let time be our partner, guiding us, uplifting us, and reminding us of the beauty in every tick and tock.

Chapter 5: Organizing Your Finances

Financial Literacy: The Basics

In the vast landscape of life, finances often resemble a dense forest—mysterious, intimidating, and teeming with both opportunities and pitfalls. Journey with Carlos, a passionate musician who, despite his talent, often found himself entangled in the thorny vines of financial woes. His earnings, sporadic and unpredictable, contrasted starkly with mounting bills and unforeseen expenses.

● Understanding Your Money: Income, Expenses, Savings

○ Carlos's first step towards financial clarity was understanding his money flow. He began by categorizing his income sources: gigs, music lessons, and occasional session recordings. Next, he listed his fixed expenses—rent, utilities, insurance—and variable ones like dining, entertainment, and equipment.

○ The revelation was stark. Carlos's expenses often outstripped his income, leading to debt. This exercise, though humbling, provided a clear picture, paving the way for informed decisions.

● The Importance of a Budget

○ With a clearer understanding of his finances, Carlos embarked on the journey of budgeting. Inspired by the 50/30/20 rule—50% for needs, 30% for wants, and 20% for savings—he tailored it to fit his unique lifestyle. This framework provided flexibility, allowing him to invest in his music while ensuring stability and future growth.

Money Management Mastery

The realm of finances, while intricate, isn't insurmountable. With the right tools, knowledge, and mindset, even the most daunting financial jungles can be navigated with grace and confidence.

● The Envelope System & Modern Alternatives

○ Drawing inspiration from age-old wisdom, Carlos adopted the Envelope System. He allocated cash in labeled envelopes for various categories—groceries, entertainment, studio time. Once an envelope was empty, no more spending occurred in that category until the next budget cycle. This tactile approach curbed impulsive purchases and fostered discipline.

○ However, in an increasingly digital age, Carlos also explored modern alternatives. Apps like YNAB (You Need A Budget) and Mint offered digital "envelopes," tracking expenses and offering insights in real-time.

● Investing Wisely: A Beginner's Guide

○ With a budding savings cushion, Carlos delved into the world of investments. Starting with low-risk options like CDs and bonds, he gradually explored stocks, mutual funds, and even dabbled in music royalties as an alternative investment. Guided by financial advisors and continuous learning, Carlos transformed from a novice to a savvy investor, ensuring his money worked as hard as he did.

● Preparing for the Unexpected: Emergency Funds & Insurance

○ Life, with its unpredictable cadence, often strikes a discordant note. Carlos, having faced equipment theft and health scares, recognized the importance of preparedness. He diligently built an emergency fund, covering 3-6 months of expenses. Additionally, he invested in health, equipment, and liability insurance, safeguarding against unforeseen calamities.

In the symphony of life, finances play a crucial melody—a tune that resonates with freedom, security, and dreams realized. As Carlos discovered, organizing one's finances isn't just about numbers; it's about crafting a future, note by note, with intention and foresight. Whether you're a seasoned maestro or a budding musician in the financial orchestra, let this chapter be your guide, leading you towards harmony, prosperity, and a life in tune with your aspirations.

Chapter 6: Organizing Your Mind & Emotions

Mindfulness & Meditation

In the bustling bazaar of life, our minds often resemble crowded marketplaces—noisy, chaotic, and teeming with myriad thoughts and emotions. Delve into the world of Aisha, a schoolteacher whose days were a whirlwind of lessons, grading, parent meetings, and personal commitments. Amidst this cacophony, she yearned for stillness, a sanctuary within her own mind.

● The Science Behind Mindfulness

○ Aisha's quest led her to the realm of mindfulness, a practice rooted in ancient wisdom yet validated by modern science. Studies from institutions like Harvard and Stanford revealed that regular mindfulness practices could rewire the brain, enhancing focus, reducing stress, and fostering emotional resilience.

○ For Aisha, this wasn't just about tranquility; it was about reclaiming her mental space, transforming it from a chaotic bazaar to a serene garden.

Simple Meditation Techniques for Beginners

○ Embarking on her mindfulness journey, Aisha explored various meditation techniques. Starting with guided sessions from apps like Headspace and Calm, she gradually ventured into breath-focused meditation and body scans.

○ Even simple practices, like the "Three Breath Pause"—taking three deep, intentional breaths whenever overwhelmed—offered Aisha pockets of peace amidst her bustling days.

Emotional Organization

Emotions, the vibrant hues that color our life's canvas, can be both invigorating and overwhelming. For Aisha, while the joys of teaching were plentiful, they were often overshadowed by stress, frustration, and self-doubt.

● Journaling for Clarity

○ Inspired by Julia Cameron's "Morning Pages," Aisha adopted the practice of daily journaling. Every morning, she'd pour her thoughts onto paper, unfiltered and uninhibited. This act, simple yet profound, became a mirror to her soul, reflecting her fears, aspirations, and innermost desires.

○ Over time, patterns emerged. Aisha recognized triggers that upset her equilibrium and moments that brought genuine joy. This self-awareness became the compass guiding her emotional journey.

● The Power of Positive Affirmations

○ To combat bouts of self-doubt, Aisha embraced positive affirmations. Phrases like "I am capable," "I am resilient," and "I am worthy" adorned her mirror, journal, and even her classroom board. These daily reminders, though subtle, began to reshape her self-perception, transforming inner critic monologues into empowering dialogues.

● Setting Boundaries: The Key to Emotional Well-being

○ A crucial revelation for Aisha was the importance of boundaries. Recognizing that she couldn't be everything for everyone, she began setting limits—be it time allocated for work, availability for meetings, or even emotional bandwidth. These boundaries, far from being restrictive, became her sanctuary, ensuring her emotional well-being wasn't compromised.

In the intricate tapestry of life, our mind and emotions are the threads that weave stories, dreams, and memories. As Aisha discovered, organizing this inner realm isn't about suppression; it's about understanding, embracing, and channeling. It's about crafting a mental sanctuary where thoughts blossom, emotions flow, and the soul finds its rhythm. Whether you're navigating the calm seas or braving emotional storms, let this chapter be your beacon, illuminating the path to inner harmony, clarity, and profound peace.

Chapter 7: Organizing Your Relationships

Personal Relationships

In the intricate dance of life, relationships form the steps, the rhythm, and the music. They are the ties that bind, the bridges between souls, and the mirrors reflecting our true selves. Journey with Rafael, a charismatic event planner, whose life was a mosaic of connections—family, friends, partners, and clients. Yet, amidst this web of relationships, he often felt adrift, yearning for depth and genuine connection.

● The Five Love Languages: Understanding & Communicating

○ Rafael's quest for deeper connections led him to Dr. Gary Chapman's "The Five Love Languages." Realizing that each individual expresses and perceives love differently—be it through Words of Affirmation, Acts of Service, Receiving Gifts, Quality Time, or Physical Touch—he began to decode the languages of his loved ones.

○ Take his relationship with his sister, Maria. While Rafael expressed love through thoughtful gifts, Maria's language was Quality Time. Recognizing this, their bond transformed, with Rafael prioritizing shared moments over material gestures.

● Time Management in Relationships: Quality vs. Quantity

○ In Rafael's bustling life, time was a precious commodity. He learned the hard way that relationships thrived not on the quantity, but the quality of time spent. His weekly coffee catchup with his best friend, Leo, transformed from distracted multitasking sessions to phone-free, heart-to-heart conversations. These intentional moments, though fewer, deepened their bond immeasurably.

Professional Relationships

Beyond personal ties, Rafael's profession demanded a plethora of professional relationships. From clients to vendors, each connection was a delicate dance of expectations, boundaries, and mutual respect.

● Networking with Purpose

○ Attending countless events, Rafael was no stranger to networking. However, he shifted from aimless mingling to purpose-driven connections. Instead of collecting business cards, he focused on genuine conversations, understanding needs, and offering value. This approach not only expanded his professional circle but also solidified his reputation as a genuine, trustworthy ally.

• The Art of Effective Communication

○ Misunderstandings with a key client taught Rafael the paramount importance of clear communication. He adopted tools like the "Two-Minute Rule" for emails—keeping them concise and to the point. For complex discussions, face-to-face meetings or video calls became his go-to, ensuring clarity and reducing misinterpretations.

○ Additionally, Rafael embraced active listening, understanding that true communication wasn't just about speaking but genuinely hearing and understanding the other party.

Relationships, as Rafael discovered, are the lifeblood of our existence. They are the melodies that enrich our days, the anchors in tumultuous times, and the mirrors reflecting our growth. Organizing relationships isn't about meticulous scheduling or strategic networking; it's about intention, understanding, and genuine connection. As we navigate the myriad relationships in our lives, this chapter serves as a guide, illuminating the path to deeper connections, meaningful interactions, and a heart brimming with love and gratitude.

Chapter 8: Organizing Your Health & Wellness

55

Physical Health

In the grand theater of life, our bodies play the lead role—a vessel that carries our dreams, aspirations, and experiences. Yet, amidst the hustle of daily life, this vessel often gets neglected. Dive into the world of Priya, a tech entrepreneur, whose days were a blur of coding, meetings, and caffeine. While her startup thrived, her health took a backseat, leading to fatigue, frequent illnesses, and a diminishing zest for life.

Meal Planning & Prepping for Nutritional Success

○ Priya's wake-up call was a health scare, prompting her to prioritize nutrition. She embarked on the journey of meal planning, dedicating Sundays to chart out balanced meals for the week. From vibrant salads to protein-packed smoothies, her menu transformed.

○ The magic, however, lay in meal prepping. Cooking in batches and using portioned containers, Priya ensured that even on her busiest days, a nutritious meal was just a microwave beep away. This shift not only enhanced her energy levels but also reduced her reliance on unhealthy takeouts.

The Importance of Regular Exercise: Finding a Routine that Works for You

○ Gym memberships and unused fitness equipment were testimonies to Priya's sporadic attempts at exercise. The change came when she realized that fitness wasn't one-size-fits-all. Instead of forcing herself into rigorous regimes, she explored different activities—yoga, dance, hiking—finally discovering a passion for kickboxing.

○ This newfound love, coupled with a community of supportive peers, made exercise a joy rather than a chore. Priya's days began with vigor, her body becoming a testament to her commitment.

Mental Health

Beyond the physical, Priya grappled with the challenges of mental well-being. The pressures of entrepreneurship, coupled with personal responsibilities, often led to sleepless nights, anxiety, and a sense of isolation.

● The Role of Sleep in Overall Well-being

○ Reading Matthew Walker's "Why We Sleep," Priya recognized the paramount importance of rest. She established a sleep routine—dimming lights, digital detox, and calming rituals like reading or chamomile tea. Over time, her sleep quality improved, leading to enhanced cognition, mood, and overall well-being.

● Stress Management Techniques

○ Entrepreneurship, with its highs and lows, brought its share of stress. Priya explored various stress-busting techniques, from deep-breathing exercises to grounding practices like the "5-4-3-2-1" method—identifying five things she could see, four she could touch, three she could hear, two she could smell, and one she could taste.

○ Additionally, she embraced therapy, finding solace in sessions that offered insights, coping mechanisms, and a safe space to express and explore.

In the intricate dance of life, health and wellness form the rhythm that guides our steps. As Priya discovered, organizing one's health isn't about stringent diets or grueling workouts; it's about listening to one's body, understanding its needs, and nurturing it with love and care. Whether you're scaling the peaks of physical challenges or navigating the depths of emotional turmoil, let this chapter be your guide, leading you towards a life of vitality, balance, and radiant well-being.

Chapter 9: Maintaining Your Organized Life

The Journey of Continuity

In the ever-evolving narrative of life, organization isn't a destination—it's a journey. It's akin to tending a garden; even after the seeds are sown and the plants bloom, they require nurturing, pruning, and care. Dive into the world of Luca, a renowned chef, who, after a whirlwind journey of organizing every facet of his life, grappled with the challenge of maintaining this newfound order.

● The Power of Habits

○ Drawing inspiration from James Clear's "Atomic Habits," Luca recognized that the bedrock of sustained organization lay in cultivating habits. Instead of grand, sweeping changes, he focused on tiny, incremental shifts. For instance, instead of an elaborate hour-long morning routine, he started with five minutes of meditation daily. This seemingly small habit, over time, expanded organically, setting a serene tone for his day.

● Regular Check-ins & Adjustments

○ Luca's restaurant menu, much like life, was dynamic. Seasonal ingredients, customer preferences, and culinary innovations meant constant evolution. Similarly, he instituted monthly "life audits"—dedicated times to assess, reflect, and recalibrate. These check-ins, be it for his finances, relationships, or personal goals, ensured that he stayed aligned with his values and aspirations.

Embracing Change & Flexibility

Life, in its unpredictable beauty, often throws curveballs—unexpected events, shifts in priorities, or new challenges. For Luca, it was the birth of his twin daughters. While this brought immense joy, it also upheaved his meticulously organized life.

● The Art of Letting Go

○ With fatherhood, Luca learned the profound art of letting go. Not every day went as planned, not every list was checked off, and that was okay. Organization, he realized, wasn't about rigid structures but about creating a flexible framework that could adapt and evolve.

● Seeking Support & Delegating

○ Running a restaurant and managing midnight baby feedings, Luca recognized he couldn't do it all. He embraced delegation, entrusting his sous-chef with greater responsibilities and seeking support from his partner and family in parenting. This not only ensured that tasks were managed but also deepened his bonds, fostering teamwork and mutual respect.

● Celebrating Small Wins

○ In the quest for organization, Luca began celebrating small victories. A successfully executed dinner service, a day without any baby meltdowns, or even a few moments of solitude became reasons for gratitude. These celebrations, though modest, fueled his motivation, reminding him of the progress made and the journey ahead.

Maintaining an organized life, as Luca discovered, is a dance—a dance of habits, adjustments, and embracing the ebb and flow of life. It's about recognizing that organization isn't a static state but a dynamic process, one that requires patience, persistence, and a generous dose of self-compassion. As you waltz through the organized pathways of your life, let this chapter be your guide, illuminating the steps, the missteps, and the beautiful journey of crafting and maintaining a life of purpose, clarity, and joy.

Chapter 10: Conclusion

71

The Symphony of an Organized Life

In the grand concert of existence, each of us is both the conductor and the lead musician, orchestrating a symphony that is uniquely ours. From the gentle melodies of daily routines to the crescendos of life's pivotal moments, organization forms the sheet music guiding our performance.

Reflect upon the journey of Elena, a documentary filmmaker. Her life, much like her films, was a tapestry of stories, emotions, and experiences. Each chapter of this book resonated with her, offering insights, tools, and perspectives that transformed her world, frame by frame.

● The Ripple Effect of Organization

○ As Elena delved into organizing her physical spaces, she noticed a ripple effect. Her clutter-free studio not only enhanced her creativity but also influenced her team's productivity and morale. The environment, once chaotic, now echoed with collaborative energy and purposeful action.

○ Similarly, as she organized her finances, the clarity and control she gained spilled over into her professional decisions. Budgeting for her projects became more streamlined, and financial discussions with stakeholders more transparent and confident.

● The Intangible Rewards

○ Beyond the tangible benefits, Elena's organized life brought forth intangible rewards. Her relationships, once taken for granted, became treasures she nurtured with time and intention. Her health, previously neglected, became a priority, enhancing her vitality and zest for life.

○ The mental peace and clarity she achieved became her compass, guiding her storytelling, influencing her film narratives, and deepening her connection with her audience.

The Ever-Evolving Journey

Life, in its infinite wisdom, is ever-evolving, ever-changing. And so is the art of organization. It's not a static achievement but a dynamic journey, adapting and growing with life's seasons.

● The Importance of Lifelong Learning

○ Elena, in her quest for stories, was a lifelong learner. She applied this ethos to her organizational journey, constantly seeking new methods, tools, and perspectives. Whether it was a new time management technique or a novel approach to emotional well-being, she remained a curious student of life.

● Embracing Imperfections

 Not every day was picture-perfect. There were missed deadlines, cluttered spaces, and emotional upheavals. Yet, Elena learned to embrace these imperfections, recognizing that they added depth and authenticity to her life's narrative. Organization, she realized, wasn't about creating a flawless tableau but about crafting a genuine, heartfelt story.

As we draw the curtains on this guide, remember that the essence of organization lies not in meticulous lists or pristine spaces. It's about crafting a life that resonates with purpose, passion, and authenticity. It's about the harmony that emerges when every note, every beat, and every pause find its rightful place in the symphony of existence.

Elena's story, and the stories of countless others woven through these pages, serve as testaments to the transformative power of organization. As you embark on your unique journey, let these tales inspire you, guide you, and remind you of the boundless possibilities that await.

Here's to the organized pathways, the melodies of order, and the beautiful symphony that is life. Let the music play on!

Bonus: Workbook

Download your FREE Companion Workbook
HERE: *https://socialobelisk.systeme.io/ lifechaos*

Appendix A: Recommended Tools & Resources

In the vast landscape of organization, tools and resources serve as the compass and map, guiding us through uncharted territories and ensuring we stay on course. This curated list, inspired by the stories and experiences shared throughout our journey, offers a treasure trove of aids designed to enhance, simplify, and elevate your organizational endeavors.

1. Physical Spaces

- **Kon Mari Method**: Marie Kondo's book, "The Life-Changing Magic of Tidying Up," offers a deep dive into the art of decluttering and organizing physical spaces.

- **Clear Storage Solutions**: Brands like The Container Store and IKEA offer a range of transparent storage options, ensuring visibility and accessibility.

- **Label Makers**: Devices like the DYMO LabelManager or Brother P-touch add clarity to storage, making item retrieval a breeze.

2. Time Management

- **Digital Calendars**: Google Calendar and Apple Calendar offer synchronization across devices, ensuring you're always updated.

- **Pomodoro Apps**: Tools like TomatoTimer or Focus Booster can help implement the Pomodoro Technique, enhancing productivity.

- **Analog Planners**: Passion Planner and Moleskine offer tactile planning experiences, merging functionality with aesthetic appeal.

3. Financial Organization

- **Budgeting Apps**: YNAB (You Need A Budget) and Mint provide real-time insights into your finances, aiding in budgeting and expense tracking.

- **Investment Platforms**: Apps like Robinhood or platforms like Vanguard offer avenues for both novice and seasoned investors.

- **Emergency Fund Trackers**: Tools like Qapital or Simple can help automate savings, ensuring you're always prepared for unforeseen expenses.

4. Mind & Emotions

- **Meditation Apps**: Headspace and Calm offer guided meditation sessions, aiding in mindfulness and mental clarity.

- **Journaling Platforms**: Day One and Penzu provide digital spaces for reflection, introspection, and emotional exploration.

- **Positive Affirmation Resources**: Louise Hay's book, "You Can Heal Your Life," offers insights into the transformative power of positive affirmations.

5. Relationships

- **Communication Tools**: Platforms like Zoom or Microsoft Teams not only cater to professional communication but can also aid in maintaining long-distance personal relationships.

- **Relationship Building Reads**: Dr. Gary Chapman's "The Five Love Languages" provides invaluable insights into understanding and nurturing relationships.

6. Health & Wellness

- **Fitness Apps**: MyFitnessPal for nutrition tracking and Fitbit for activity monitoring can be instrumental in maintaining physical health.

- **Mental Well-being Platforms**: Talkspace and BetterHelp offer online therapy options, ensuring mental health support is always accessible.

- **Sleep Aids**: Books like "Why We Sleep" by Matthew Walker provide insights into the importance of rest, while apps like Sleep Cycle can help monitor and improve sleep patterns.

As you navigate the multifaceted realms of organization, let these tools and resources be your allies, enhancing your journey and ensuring each step is taken with confidence, clarity, and purpose. Remember, the right tool can transform a task from a challenge into a joy. Here's to organized pathways, streamlined processes, and a life enriched by the magic of order!

Appendix B: Quick Tips & Tricks Cheat Sheet

In the grand tapestry of organization, sometimes all we need is a quick glance—a swift reminder of the golden nuggets that can transform chaos into clarity. This cheat sheet, distilled from the wisdom of our journey, offers bite-sized tips and tricks designed to infuse your days with order, purpose, and joy.

1. Physical Spaces

- **Touch Once Rule**: When you pick something up, decide its fate then and there—use it, store it, or discard it.

- **Vertical Storage**: Maximize space by thinking upwards. Wall-mounted shelves and over-the-door organizers can be game-changers.

- **Color Coding**: Use colors to categorize and quickly identify items, be it files, clothing, or kitchenware.

2. Time Management

• **The Two-Minute Rule**: If a task takes less than two minutes, do it immediately.

• **Time Blocking**: Allocate specific blocks of time for tasks, ensuring focused and productive sessions.

• **BED Technique for Tasks**: **B**reak tasks down, **E**stablish priorities, **D**o one thing at a time.

3. Financial Organization

● **Pay Yourself First**: Before any expenses, allocate a portion of your income to savings.

● **Envelope System**: Allocate cash for specific categories. When it's gone, it's gone—until the next budget cycle.

● **Regular Financial Check-ins**: Dedicate time each month to review and adjust your budget.

4. Mind & Emotions

- **Three Breath Pause**: Feeling overwhelmed? Take three deep breaths to center yourself.

- **Gratitude Journal**: End each day by noting three things you're grateful for.

- **Digital Detox**: Dedicate an hour before sleep without screens to ensure restful slumber.

5. Relationships

- **Active Listening**: When conversing, be fully present. Listen more than you speak.

- **Regular Check-ins**: Dedicate time for regular heart-to-hearts with loved ones, ensuring the bond remains strong.

- **Quality Over Quantity**: Prioritize meaningful interactions over frequent, superficial ones.

6. Health & Wellness

- **Hydration Reminder**: Set hourly reminders to drink water, ensuring you stay hydrated.

- **Move Every Hour**: A quick stretch or a short walk can boost energy and focus.

- **Mindful Eating**: Savor each bite, appreciating the flavors and textures, and recognizing when you're full.

As you navigate the myriad avenues of organization, let this cheat sheet be your compass—a swift, accessible guide ensuring you stay on course. Whether you're amidst the daily hustle or facing unexpected challenges, these quick tips and tricks are your allies, infusing each moment with clarity, purpose, and a touch of magic. Here's to organized days, streamlined processes, and a life brimming with intention and joy!

Appendix C: Inspirational Quotes on Organization

In the vast expanse of organization, sometimes all we need is a beacon—a guiding light that illuminates our path, inspires our spirit, and fuels our journey. This collection of quotes, handpicked from the annals of wisdom, offers a reservoir of inspiration, reminding us of the profound beauty and power of organization.

1. **"For every minute spent organizing, an hour is earned."** - *Benjamin Franklin*
2. **"The secret of getting ahead is getting started. The secret of getting started is breaking your complex overwhelming tasks into small manageable tasks and starting on the first one."** - *Mark Twain*
3. **"Organizing is what you do before you do something, so that when you do it, it's not all mixed up."** - *A.A. Milne*
4. **"Simplicity is the ultimate sophistication."** - *Leonardo da Vinci*
5. **"Clutter is nothing more than postponed decisions."** - *Barbara Hemphill*
6. **"The key is not to prioritize what's on your schedule, but to schedule your priorities."** - *Stephen R. Covey*
7. **"Out of clutter, find simplicity. From discord, find harmony. In the middle of difficulty lies opportunity."** - *Albert Einstein*
8. **"Have nothing in your house that you do not know to be useful or believe to be beautiful."** - *William Morris*
9. **"Organization isn't about perfection; it's about efficiency, reducing stress and clutter, saving time and money, and improving your overall quality of life."** - *Christina Scalise*
10. **"Order is the sanity of the mind, the health of the body,**

the peace of the soul, and the fuel of life." - *Anonymous*

11. **"The achievement of one's goal is assured the moment one commits oneself."** - *Napoleon Hill*

12. **"The space in which we live should be for the person we are becoming now, not for the person we were in the past."** - *Marie Kondo*

13. **"Organize your life around your dreams – and watch them come true."** - *Unknown*

14. **"Eliminate physical clutter. More importantly, eliminate spiritual clutter."** - *D.H. Mondfleur*

15. **"The best way to get something done is to begin."** - *Unknown*

As you traverse the pathways of organization, let these words be your guiding stars, illuminating the beauty of order, the joy of simplicity, and the profound peace that arises from a life well-organized. Whether you're taking the first step or are miles into your journey, these quotes serve as gentle reminders of the transformative power of organization—a force that shapes dreams, crafts realities, and weaves the tapestry of a life lived with purpose and passion.

Don't miss out!

Visit the website below and you can sign up to receive emails whenever Sue Neumann publishes a new book. There's no charge and no obligation.

https://books2read.com/r/B-A-XUMGB-VOIAF

BOOKS 2 READ

Connecting independent readers to independent writers.

www.ingramcontent.com/pod-product-compliance
Lightning Source LLC
Chambersburg PA
CBHW051237160726

47994CB00002B/920